The Education Center, Inc.'s

Bulletin Boards For Busy Teachers

Grades K–6

D1315692

Editors:
Rebecca S. Andrews
Lynn B. Coble

Artists:
Cathie Carter
Jennifer Tipton

Cover Designer:
Charlene Shidisky

How To Use This Book

Today's busy teachers have unbelievable demands on their time. Bulletin boards can become burdens rather than invaluable teaching tools. *Bulletin Boards For Busy Teachers* was designed for the teacher who wants an attractive and stimulating classroom environment without spending hours of scarce time.

Within these pages, you'll find almost 100 easy-to-make displays designed by teachers like yourself. All of the displays involve students and invite their participation. The book is divided into four sections: Fall, Winter, Spring, and Anytime. You'll find a display for every season and holiday, plus plenty of ideas to use anytime of the year.

Each bulletin board is fully illustrated and includes complete instructions for the teacher. Patterns to reproduce or enlarge are also included to make your job easier. And, to give your bulletin boards that special touch that makes them stand out in a crowd, we've included suggestions for ways to incorporate 3-D elements in many of the displays.

Copyright 1992 by The Education Center, Inc., 1607 Battleground Avenue, Greensboro, NC 27408. All rights reserved except as here noted. Permission is granted to reproduce pages for individual classroom use only and not for resale or distribution. Reproduction for an entire school or school system is prohibited.

Table Of Contents

Our thanks to the following contributors to this book: Diane Afferton, Diane Badden, Susan Barnett, Carolyn Barwick, Lois Benedict, Cheryl Blanchi, Deborah Boehm, Fay Bowen, Janice Bradley, Vivian N. Campbell, Marla Crisman, Diana Curtis, Kathleen Darby, Julie Eick, Jo Farrimond, Jennifer Gardner, Mary K. Good, Rebecca Webster Graves, Sharon Haley, Charlotte Hall, Paula Holdren, Valerie Hornbaker, Beth Jones, Laurie Kin, Dianne Knight, Lillian Krause, Dianne Krieser, Bonnie jo Kyles, Vivian N. Lynn, Pamela McKedy, Linda Nelson, Julie S. Polak, Don Reiffenberger, Danette Rutherford, Teena Sand, Cheryl Seachord, Connie Stark, Sandra Steen, Sarah Steinwand, Ellie Sulcer, Sandra Taylor, Arnetra Terry, Tanya Wilder, Sally Williams, Carolyn Wojtera.

Here's a bright idea to welcome your new batch of students! Bring several old pairs of sunglasses to school. On the first day, photograph students in groups of two or three wearing the sunglasses. Duplicate the sunglasses pattern on page 51 on different colors of construction paper for students to cut out. Attach the photographs to the sunglasses patterns; then mount them on the board with a large cut-out sun.

Let new students know that you're glad they'll be "hanging around" your class this year! Duplicate the T-shirt pattern on page 53 on white construction paper for each child. Have the student cut out, personalize, and decorate his shirt. Use a permanent marker to label a white, cotton T-shirt as shown. Display the shirts using clothespins and lengths of heavy string or plastic clothesline. (For a variation of this idea, see page 6.)

Start the year on a "beary" positive note! Duplicate the teddy bear pattern on page 55 on construction paper for each child. Cut out and label each bear with a student's name. Also cut out a speech bubble from white paper for each student. Mount the bears and speech bubbles as shown on the bulletin board. Later in the week have each child tell about one thing that makes him special. Write his comment in the speech bubble above his bear.

Welcome students to your "pad" with this cheerful display. Enlarge the frog pattern on page 57; then color it, cut it out, and mount it on the board. (For a 3-D touch, glue a piece of sponge to the back of the frog; then glue the sponge to the bulletin board.) Duplicate the lily pad pattern on page 57 onto green construction paper for each child. Cut out each lily pad. Ask children to bring in photos of themselves to mount on the lily pads. What a "hoppy" way to say hello!

Plant Yourself Here!

Mount a red-checkered, paper tablecloth onto the bottom half of a bulletin board. Duplicate the patterns on page 59 onto colorful construction paper for each child. After cutting out the patterns, label each flower with a student's name; then attach it to a green pipe cleaner. Tape the pipe cleaner to the back of a flowerpot. Staple the flowerpots onto the board, bending the pipe cleaners slightly so that the flowers appear 3-D. On a table positioned under the display, place a small potted plant for each child. On the first day of school, have students go to the board and label their flowerpots with favorite hobbies, book titles, etc.

The beginning of a new year is the perfect time to remind students to "try a little tenderness." Mount a gift-wrapped box on a bulletin board as shown. On the first day of school, discuss with students how they can be considerate of each other so that everyone is "handled with care." Finish the discussion by having each child trace her hand on colorful construction paper. After cutting out her tracing, have the student label it with her name and staple it to the board.

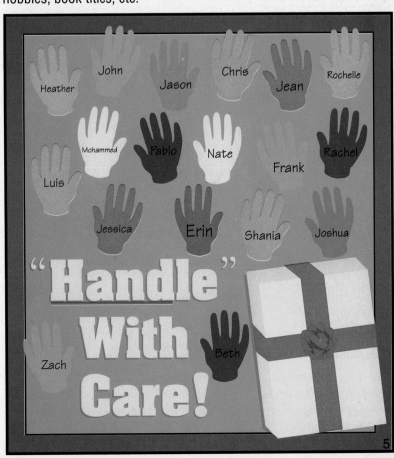

It Was A "Tee-rific" Summer!

Enjoy favorite summer memories with this student-made display. Duplicate a T-shirt pattern (page 53) on white paper for each student. After cutting out his pattern, the student decorates it with pictures to illustrate his favorite activities of the summer. Mount finished shirts on the board. Choose several children each day to explain the pictures on their shirts. (For a variation of this idea, see the bulletin board on page 3.)

I Can't Forget Summer! Can You?

NICOLE
I visited my cousins in Florida.

DEVON
I went to soccer camp.

JODY
I rode a great roller coaster!

RICKI
I skated every day.

BOBBI
I learned to knit.

LEAH
My family went to the Grand Canyon.

SHARNELLE
I took an art class.

To make this memorable display, enlarge the elephant pattern on page 61. Color and cut out the elephant; then staple it to the board, leaving the trunk unstapled. Gently curl the trunk around a pencil; then tie a bright piece of ribbon around the trunk. Have each student cut a cloud shape from colorful construction paper. Students label their clouds with their names and sentences describing favorite summer memories. Add the clouds to the display.

Doing A Whale Of A Job!

Students will do a whale of a job when you use this fun jobs bulletin board! Label colorful whale cutouts with students' names. Label white spout cutouts with classroom jobs. (See the whale and spout patterns on page 63.) Attach several rows of blue corrugated border for water. Change the whales weekly.

With this fun display, everyone will be eager to "pitch in" to keep your classroom running smoothly. For each classroom job, duplicate the baseball glove pattern on page 65 on brown construction paper. Cut out the gloves and label them with jobs. Duplicate the baseball pattern on page 65 on white paper for each student. Cut out the baseballs and label them with students' names. For an interesting border, mount baseball cards around the edges of the board.

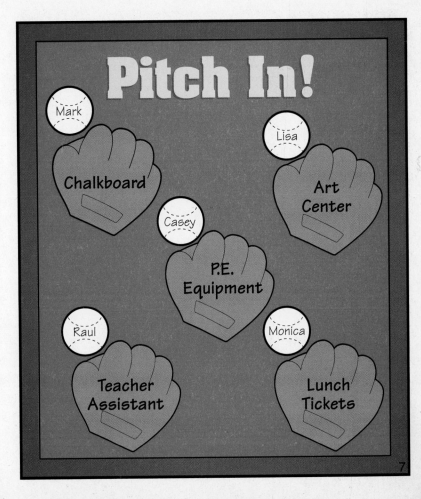

An
Autumn Rainbow
Of Great Work

Somewhere over the rainbow there's a great way to display fall's finest work! Duplicate the leaf patterns on page 67 on red, yellow, and orange construction paper. Have students cut out the leaves, then mount them on the board in a rainbow shape as shown. Next have each child choose a favorite paper to mount on a piece of construction paper and display on the board. Now wasn't that easy?

Poppin' Good Papers!

Did you know that October is National Popcorn Poppin' Month? Enlarge the popcorn popper on page 69; then color it, cut it out, and mount it on the board. Duplicate the paper topper (page 69) on white paper for each child. Have students color the edges of their toppers with yellow crayons before cutting out the patterns and slitting them on the dotted lines. After each child has mounted a favorite paper on construction paper, have him slip his topper on the corner of his paper. For fun, pop some popcorn in class and have students glue the popped kernels to the background of the board.

Check These Out!

Checkerboard patterns create a flashy fall bulletin board! Cut a tree trunk out of brown butcher paper. Or crumple brown paper bags and glue them to the board in a tree shape. Have students use markers to color sheets of one-inch graph paper in checkerboard patterns. Each child traces a leaf pattern (see page 67) onto his checkerboard pattern; then he cuts out his leaf and staples it to the tree. Add favorite papers mounted on construction paper for everyone to "check out."

Send self-esteem skyrocketing this fall! Enlarge, color, cut out, and mount the squirrel pattern on page 71. Duplicate the nut pattern on page 73 on light brown construction paper for each student. Choose one child each week to honor on the board. Have each of the child's classmates cut out his nut pattern and label it with a compliment about the week's special person; then post the cutouts on the board. Send the compliments home at the end of the week, stapled together to make a personal praise booklet!

Our Favorite Monster

What could be spookier this Halloween than a one-of-a-kind monster? Assign a body section (head, body, an arm, a leg) to each of six teams. Challenge each team to use construction paper and other art materials to make its body part. Remind students that no peeking at the other teams' designs is allowed. (Give approximate sizes to teams before beginning.) After the monster has been assembled on the board, let the class name their Halloween creation. Then have each student write a story about the monster and its monstrously amazing abilities!

Haunted Helpers

This easy-to-make management tool doubles as a spooky seasonal display! Enlarge the tombstone pattern on page 75; then duplicate it onto gray construction paper (one copy for each classroom job). Enlarge the ghost pattern on page 75; then duplicate it onto white paper. Laminate and cut out the patterns. Program the tombstones and ghosts with a wipe-off marker. Rotate your haunted helpers daily by wiping the ghosts clean and relabeling them.

Looking for an easy Halloween art project? Have students cut out eyes, noses, mouths, ears, and other facial features from old magazines. Duplicate the pumpkin on page 77 on orange paper for each child. After cutting out his pumpkin, the student glues facial features onto his cutout to create an out-of-the-ordinary pumpkin personality. Glue a small piece of sponge to the back of each pumpkin; then glue the sponge piece to the bulletin board to give a 3-D effect. There never was a pumpkin patch quite like this one!

Whoooo Knows These?

A moaning ghost wants to question your students this Halloween! Cut out a ghost's head and hands from white paper; then attach them to the top of a bulletin board as shown. Cut out, label, and mount a speech bubble as shown. Label colorful tagboard strips with questions about a book your students are reading, math problems, or scrambled spelling words. Change the strips frequently.

nrdife

uebsace

vmeio

febero

elpope

A Bird Of A Different Feather

Students will be as proud as they can be when they create this fine-feathered friend! Staple a large brown circle to a bulletin board. Show students how to wrap a small piece of brown tissue paper around the eraser end of a pencil, dip it in glue, and attach it to the circle. After students have completely covered the circle using this technique, attach paper feet and a smaller brown circle decorated as a turkey's face. Have each student bring a colorful sock from home. Pin the socks to the board for turkey feathers of a different kind!

Each one of you is special.
I know that to be true.
And that is why I want to say,
"I'm so thankful for you!"

I'm Thankful For You!

Ted
Deanna
Ty
Josh
Kim
Zach
Keesha
Amy
Beth
Tony
Troy

Show students you care with a heartwarming seasonal display. Enlarge the cornucopia pattern on page 79; then color it, cut it out, and mount it on the board. Write the poem shown on the cornucopia, adding a class photo if desired. Have each student make a construction paper fruit or vegetable cutout, label it with his name, and add it to the display.

Let this turkey talk your students into being on their best behavior during November! Enlarge the turkey pattern on page 81. Color and cut out the turkey; then mount it on the board with the poem. Cut out and display enlarged paper feathers (pattern on page 81) in a pocket as shown. Each time good behavior is exhibited by the entire class, staple a feather to the turkey. When all of the feathers have been added to ol' Tom, treat students to a popcorn party!

Count your blessings one by one with this fun display! Duplicate the calculator pattern on page 83 on construction paper for each child. After cutting out his calculator, have each student label its window with something that he is thankful for. As a finishing touch, the student draws and cuts out a picture of his face and a pair of hands; then he glues them to the calculator as shown.

'Twas The Night Before Christmas...

The beauty of this bulletin board is in its no-patterns-necessary construction. Have each student cut a house shape from purple construction paper. Students cut window and door shapes from yellow construction paper and draw a holiday decoration on each; then they glue the cutouts to the houses. Using dots punched from various colors of paper, have students decorate green construction-paper trees to add to the display. Complete the effect with a generous application of aerosol "snow."

Spread the spirit of giving with this attractive display. Have each child trace a large heart (pattern on page 85) onto a sheet of holiday gift wrap and cut it out. On the back of a small index card, have the student write about a gift he can give that doesn't cost any money—a gift from the heart. The student glues his card in the center of his heart. Display the hearts on a background of bright foil wrapping paper for a display that shines with the spirit of giving.

"...And A Partridge In A Pear Tree"

A towering tree of characters from "The Twelve Days Of Christmas" makes for one lively display! Duplicate the patterns on pages 87–93 on white construction paper; then have students color, decorate, and cut out the characters for you. If desired, let students add special touches with sequins, glitter, felt, fabric trim, and other materials for a smashing portrayal of this favorite song.

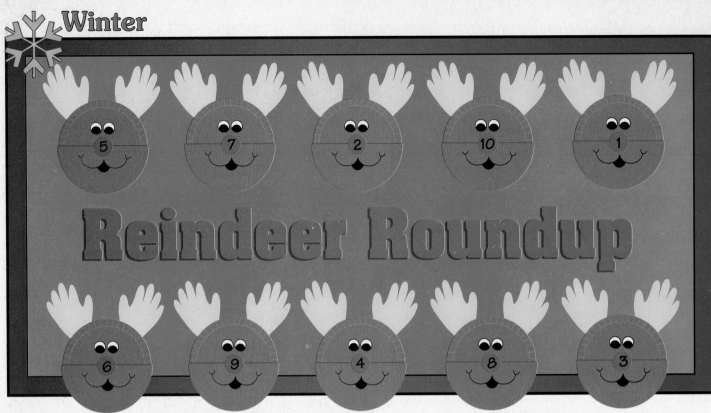

Reindeer Roundup

A herd of reindeer can help your students practice math facts this Christmas! Have students paint 15 white paper plates with brown paint. After drying, cut five of the plates in half. Staple each half to an uncut plate to make a pocket. Glue two hand tracings cut from yellow paper to each plate as shown. Add large wiggle eyes and a red nose labeled with a number. During free time, students label slips of paper with math facts and place them in the correct pockets. At the end of the day, take the facts from one reindeer and have the class check them for accuracy.

What's Under The Tree For Me?

What's under the tree for me? Give each child two squares, one cut from holiday gift wrap and one cut from white paper. On the white paper, have the student draw a picture of a gift she hopes to receive this holiday season. The child decorates her wrapping paper square with a construction-paper bow or ribbon; then she staples this square to the top of her drawing. Place the gifts around a large paper tree which the class has decorated using paper scraps and other materials.

Invite your students to visit Santa's workshop during their free time this holiday season. Enlarge, color, and cut out the Santa pattern on page 95; then mount Santa on the board. Glue a number 1–4, cut from gift wrap, to each of four large manila envelopes. Stuff the envelopes with holiday puzzles, word scrambles, coloring pages, and other fun activities; then staple the envelopes to the board. Include an extra envelope to hold answer keys so that students can check their work.

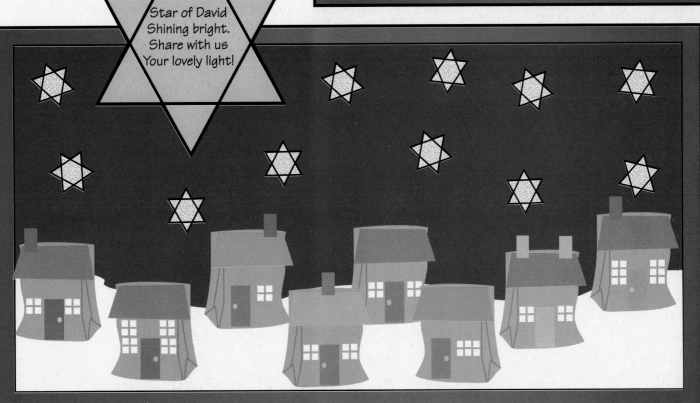

Star of David
Shining bright.
Share with us
Your lovely light!

Create a lovely nighttime scene to celebrate Hanukkah. Enlarge the large Star of David pattern on page 97 on yellow or gold paper. Cut it out and label it with the poem shown; then attach it to the board. Have each child cut out a duplicated copy of the smaller star (page 97), cover it with gold glitter, and mount it on the board. Have students decorate small paper sacks to look like houses; then have the children stuff the sacks with newspaper and add construction paper roofs. Pin the completed houses on the board to make a 3-D village beneath the starry sky.

Putting Our Best Foot Forward In 1993!

Start the new year off on the right foot! Cut out a large footprint from bulletin board paper; then add large wiggle eyes and a mouth. Mount the footprint on the board. Have each student stand in his stocking feet on a 9" X 12" sheet of colorful construction paper, bend over, and trace his footprint with a pencil. After cutting out his footprint, the student labels it with a New Year's resolution. Post the footprints on the board. For an interesting border, try pinning colorful shoelaces around the board's edges.

What are your students' wishes for the new year? Find out by enlarging, coloring, cutting out, labeling, and mounting the singing star pattern on page 99. Add several cut-out musical notes to the display. Duplicate the blank star on page 101 on yellow paper for each child. Have students label the stars with their wishes for the new year, then cut them out. Post the stars around the board's edges.

Light A Candle For Peace

Celebrate Dr. Martin Luther King, Jr.'s birthday in January with this thought-provoking bulletin board. Enlarge the silhouette of Dr. King on page 103; then cut it out and mount it on the board. With students, discuss Dr. King's life and his work for equality and peace. To follow up the discussion, have each child cut a rectangle from light blue construction paper and label it with his name and a wish for peace. The student then glues a yellow paper flame to the rectangle as shown.

They Made Their Mark!

Spotlight famous African Americans during Black History Month. Duplicate the target pattern on page 105 on white paper for each child to color and cut out. Next have each child research a famous African American and write a paragraph or sentence about the person on his pattern. Duplicate the arrow pattern on page 105 on construction paper for each child. Have students label the arrows with the names of their famous people. Pin the arrows near the matching targets on the board. After students have discussed the famous people, remove the arrows. Challenge students to match each arrow to the correct target.

Invite Warmhearted Willie into your classroom during the blustery months. Attach student-made snowflakes in clusters to form a snowman shape. Complete the effect with a construction paper hat, mittens, a heart, facial features, and the poem on a speech bubble.

Here's a bulletin board that will warm up winter doldrums! Enlarge the pattern on page 107 to make the display's character. Post several index cards labeled with winter story starters. Duplicate the mitten pattern on page 109 on white paper for each child. After writing his story on the cutout, a student glues it to a piece of colorful paper and cuts around it, leaving a border of color. Post the mittens along with student-made snowflakes.

Round, jolly snowmen decorate this winter display! Have each child glue together three white paper loops. Students decorate their snowmen with paper scraps before pinning them to the board. Add a large snowman cutout and student-made snowflakes to the display.

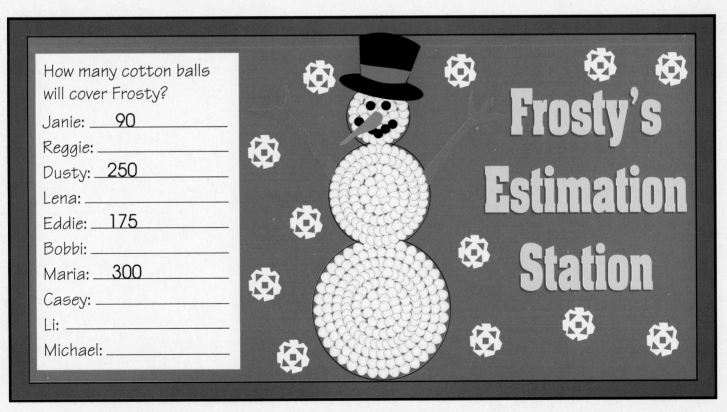

How many cotton balls will cover Frosty?

Janie: _____90_____

Reggie: _____

Dusty: _____250_____

Lena: _____

Eddie: _____175_____

Bobbi: _____

Maria: _____300_____

Casey: _____

Li: _____

Michael: _____

Frosty's Estimation Station

Divide a bulletin board into three sections. In the middle section, draw the outline of a snowman. Add a class list and title as shown. Have students estimate the number of cotton balls needed to completely cover Frosty and write their estimates on the list. During free time, let small groups glue cotton balls onto the snowman. Count the total and compare it to the estimates. Reward the child with the closest estimate. Then add paper features to the snowman and student-made snowflakes to the display.

Spread the message of love with a simple, yet memorable, bulletin board. Cut a large heart from tagboard and mount it on a board. During free time, have students cut pictures of children from old magazines and glue them to the heart, collage-fashion, until it is completely covered. Add a border of smaller hearts (patterns on page 111) decorated with student photos.

Who do you call when there's a problem? The Love Bug, that's who! Have students share about times when the Love Bug (disguised as kindness, love, and understanding) helped them out of a sticky situation. After the discussion, give each student a white doily placemat and a copy of the heart pattern on page 85. Have the student trace the heart pattern on light pink paper and cut it out; then, on the pink heart, have her write a story about a time when she was rescued by the Love Bug. Glue finished stories on the placemats and trim them. For fun, let students add red finger-print Love Bugs to their stories.

How About A Sweetheart Shake?

70
- 49
1.

40
- 21
2.

20
- 18
3.

50
- 38
4.

60
- 45
5.

70
- 33
6.

80
- 16
7.

90
- 44
8.

40
- 13
9.

50
- 34
10.

60
- 49
11.

30
- 18
12.

Use the cupid pattern on page 113 and the heart pattern on page 85 to create this Valentine's Day scene. Enlarge, color, cut out, and mount the cupid. Duplicate 12 copies of the heart pattern on pink or red paper. After cutting out the hearts, label them with math problems and number them 1–12. Each child who correctly answers a designated number of problems on her paper is rewarded with a Sweetheart Shake. To make a shake, blend vanilla ice cream, milk, mint extract, and red food coloring. To vary the display, laminate the hearts and reprogram them with new problems each day until February 14. Award a shake to those children who have attempted all of the problems.

My Class Has A Lot Of Heart!

A flowerpot of personalized hearts tells your students that they are special on Valentine's Day and every day of the year! Attach small cut-out hearts (patterns on page 111) labeled with student names to thick green pipe cleaners. Label a large flowerpot cutout (enlarge the pattern on page 59) as shown and staple it to the board for a pocket. Insert the hearts' "stems" in the flowerpot pocket for a display that's full of heart!

Good For "Ewe"!

Make students' work the focal point of a simple, spring bulletin board. Mat students' work onto red construction paper. Enlarge the sheep pattern on page 115 to add to the board. During free time, let students glue cotton to the sheep for a fluffy, 3-D effect.

Cackle, cackle, cluck, cluck! This cheerful chick creates quite a spectacle as her mound of eggs grows higher and higher. Enlarge the hen and nest patterns on page 117. After coloring and cutting out the patterns, mount them on the board. Duplicate a supply of construction paper eggs. Explain to students that they will earn an egg for each book that they read. Challenge the class to raise the hen to the ceiling. When the hen reaches this monumental height, surprise students with an "egg-ceptional" treat!

Reading
Is "Toad-ally" Awesome!

Max's First Word

Millions Of Cats

Bea And Mr. Jones

Bedtime For Frances

Summer Business

Blueberries For Sal

The Biggest Bear

Babushka

Sweet Touch

Dawn

Motivate springtime reading with the aid of some "toad-ally" awesome helpers! Enlarge the toad pattern on page 119 to mount on the board. Also duplicate several copies of the pattern on green construction paper. When a student finishes a book he'd like to recommend to others, have him write its title on a toad pattern, cut out the pattern, and add it to the board.

Spring Is In The Air!

Welcome spring with the fluttering of butterfly wings! Duplicate the butterfly wings on page 121 on white or pastel construction paper for each child. After cutting out his wings, have the student glue three large black pom-poms in the center to make the butterfly's body. Have students color their wings with unique designs. Next have each child bend a small black pipe cleaner in half and tape it to the back of the butterfly for antennae. Fold the wings of each butterfly slightly on the dotted lines before pinning the butterflies fluttering above large tissue-paper flowers.

Books Take You Over The Rainbow

Little House In The Big Woods

Imogene's Antlers

The Patchwork Quilt

The Mother's Day Mice

The Boxcar Children

The Polar Express

Cock-A-Doodle Dudley

Share the magic of books with this bright St. Patrick's Day display. Enlarge the pot-of-gold pattern on page 123 on black paper. Cut it out and mount it on the board. Cut out a cloud shape from white paper and glue fluffy cotton around its edges. Label and mount as shown. After a child has read a new book, have her write its title on a colorful cut-out heart (patterns on page 111) and add it to the rainbow. Complete the display with student-made book jackets.

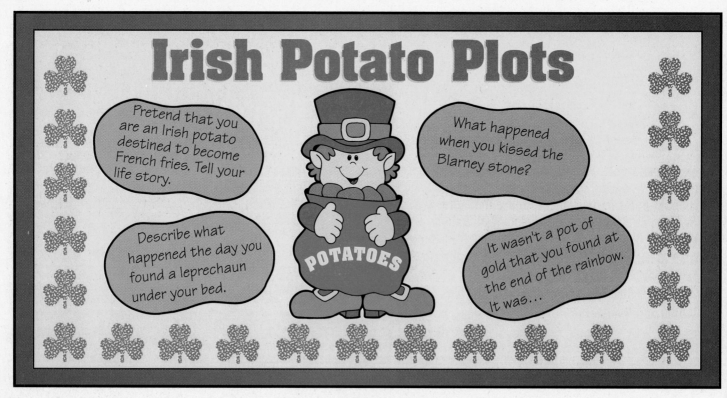

Irish Potato Plots

Pretend that you are an Irish potato destined to become French fries. Tell your life story.

What happened when you kissed the Blarney stone?

Describe what happened the day you found a leprechaun under your bed.

POTATOES

It wasn't a pot of gold that you found at the end of the rainbow. It was...

Creative writing will appear like magic with this fun display! Enlarge, color, and cut out the leprechaun pattern on page 125. Mount it on the board. Duplicate four copies of the potato pattern on page 127 on brown paper. Cut out each potato and label it with a St. Patrick's Day story starter. Have students write their stories on white copies of the potato pattern. Bind finished stories between two potato covers to make a class booklet. For a fun touch, have students sponge paint a pretty shamrock border.

Give self-esteem an "egg-stra" push! Enlarge and color the eggshell and chick patterns on page 129. Have each student decorate the top and bottom edges of a large construction-paper egg. Each day of the Easter month, draw the name of a student. Have his classmates verbally share positive attributes of the honored child as you write them on his egg.

Look what's hopping down the bunny trail! For each child, duplicate two copies of each of the bunny ear patterns on page 131 on white and pink construction paper. Have students glue the patterns together to make ears as shown. Mount copies of students' original Easter stories on pink rectangles, stapling two ears at the top of each rectangle. For a finishing touch, glue a fluffy cotton tail at the bottom of each story.

Here's a bulletin board that will brighten any room during April's rainy days! Enlarge, color, and cut out the umbrella pattern on page 133; then staple it on the board and add a brown paper handle. Duplicate the flower pattern on page 59 on white paper. Have students color and cut out their flowers; then staple them as a border on the board. Finally have students label large cut-out raindrops with haiku or sentences about rain. Pin the raindrops to the board.

Celebrate Earth Day with a display that will spur everyone to take care of our planet! Have several students paint a large white circle to resemble the earth. Mount it on the board. Have each child trace his hand onto a colorful piece of construction paper and cut it out. On the hand cutout, the student writes a sentence telling one thing he and his family can do to protect the earth and its resources. Staple the hand cutouts to the board.

It's Been A "Bee-utiful" Year!

Everyone will be buzzing about what a great school year it was with this eye-catching display! Duplicate the bee pattern on page 133 on yellow paper for each child. After cutting out his bee, have each student label it with a sentence describing a favorite memory of the school year. Post the bees above a garden of student-made flowers for a colorful finish to a great year!

This cheerful display guarantees that the last week of school will be unforgettable! Label each of five paper strips with an end-of-the-year surprise such as lunch outdoors, a popcorn party, or a video. Place each strip inside a balloon; then inflate the balloons. On a bulletin board, display a character (pattern on page 135) holding five balloon strings. Attach the inflated balloons to the ends of the strings. Pop a balloon each morning of the last five school days and enjoy the resulting surprise that day.

Let's End The Year With A BANG!

Remember the good times of the school year with a scrumptious display! Cut a large basket shape from bulletin board paper. To make a woven basket, fold the cutout in half and cut several horizontal slits on the fold; then unfold the basket and weave paper strips through the slits. Attach the ends of each strip to the back of the cutout. Duplicate the apple pattern on page 137 on red, yellow, and green paper (one apple per child). Have each student cut out his apple and label it with his favorite school memory. Finish the apples by gluing on green paper leaves.

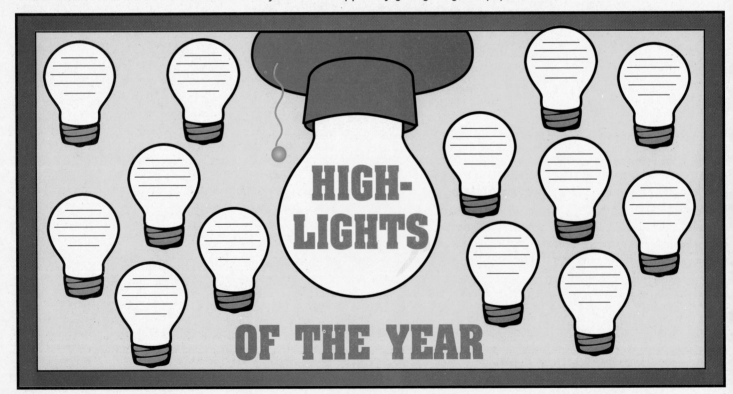

Shine a light on the bright moments of the year! Enlarge the light bulb pattern on page 139 on white paper; then cut it out. Mount the bulb on the board, adding a paper base at the top. If desired, tie a bead to the end of a piece of yarn; then attach it to the light's base as shown. Duplicate the light bulb pattern on white paper for each child. Each student cuts out her light bulb, then labels it with a sentence or paragraph describing her favorite highlight of the year.

Here's a colorful way to boost reading any time of the year! Duplicate the crayon box pattern on page 141 on orange paper for each child. Have children cut out the boxes, label them with their names, and slit them on the dotted lines. Staple the boxes to the board with a key as shown. Duplicate the crayon patterns (page 141) on red, yellow, green, and blue paper; then cut out the crayons. When a student reads a book from one of the categories, he earns an appropriately colored crayon to place in his box. The goal is to gain a crayon of each color. Use this idea to motivate other behaviors as well.

Use this eye-catching display to announce good news about your students. Enlarge, color, and cut out the pattern on page 143. Mount the pattern and a large, labeled grocery bag as shown. Each time a student has an achievement or exciting news he'd like to share, he writes it on a small, colorful index card; then he staples it to the display. Students will love "paws-ing" to read the good news!

Start with a magic dot.
Tell me what you see.
You will be amazed
At what a dot can be!

Dots, dots, and more dots make this colorful display something special! Cover a bulletin board with paper; then have students dip the eraser ends of pencils in colorful ink pads and cover the background with dots. Mount the poem as shown. To motivate writing, draw a large dot on the chalkboard and have children brainstorm what it might be: the wheel of a magic vehicle, a flower's center, a dot on a clown's suit, etc. Have each child stick a self-sticking dot on a piece of story paper. With crayons, he completes his picture around the dot and writes a story about it.

Encourage students to assist the post office by addressing this giant envelope! Post a large, laminated envelope cutout as shown. For each student, duplicate the house pattern on page 145 and label it with his address. Complete the bulletin board with a Ziploc bag containing a cloth and a wipe-off marker. For practice, students take turns locating their addresses and copying them on the large envelope with the wipe-off marker.

"Fan-tastic" Work!

Focus on your students' "fan-tastic" work with this delightful display. Enlarge, color, cut out, and post the pattern on page 147. Have each child make a fan by accordion folding a small square of wallpaper and stapling the folds at one end together. Post each fan with a favorite paper selected by the child. Now isn't that fantastic?

It never fails. No matter how well you plan, there's always at least one student who finishes early and says, "What do I do now?" Solve this dilemma with a simple display. Enlarge, color, cut out, and post the clock pattern on page 149. Beside the cutout, post a laminated piece of poster board. On the poster, use a wipe-off marker to list activities that students can do in their free time. Wipe it clean when you want to change the list.

Some Extra Time?

Try these!

1. Bulletin board activities

2. Journal

3. Math incentives

4. Folders

5. Basic skills packets

6. Read library book

7. Vocabulary cards

8. Read today's newspaper

Use this bulletin board to increase career awareness in your classroom. Duplicate the patterns on page 153 on yellow paper. Cut out the patterns. Label each receiver with a career. Label each phone with a need that requires the help of a particular worker. Attach a piece of magnetic tape to the back of each receiver; then glue a paper clip to the top of each telephone cutout. Store the receivers in a pocket stapled to the board. Have students "dial" the correct persons for assistance by matching the receivers to the telephones.

Keep students on target with a little help from Robin Hood himself! Enlarge, color, cut out, and post the Robin Hood pattern on page 151. Duplicate the arrow pattern (also on page 151) on colorful construction paper for each child. Cut out each arrow; then cut it in half. Post the arrows as shown with favorite papers selected by your students.

Encourage your active bunch to follow playground safety rules. Enlarge the monkey pattern on page 155; then color, cut out, and mount the monkey on the board with paper branches and leaves as shown. After discussing playground safety rules, have each child illustrate one of the rules. Mount the drawings on green or purple paper. Duplicate the paper topper on page 155 for each child on white paper. Have students color and cut out the toppers; then have them slit on the dotted lines and slip the toppers on the corners of their drawings.

Don't Monkey Around!
Let's play safe.

Flying High With Spelling

Spelling scores will soar with this motivating, year-round display. Cut out, label, and post a large cloud shape as shown. Duplicate the plane pattern on page 157 on colorful construction paper for each child. Have students label the planes with their names and cut them out. Students with improved spelling scores on the weekly test are allowed to post their planes "up in the air" until the next week's test.

Goody, Goody Gumball!

It's Your Birthday!

Dave 10-6
Susan 6-11
Megan 12-24
Cody 4-16
Kevin 7-10
Cary 3-29
Todd 9-30
Beth 2-23
Zach 7-4
Julie 1-14
Kim 11-3
Tina 10-11
Mike 3-12
Seth 8-9

This smiling gumball machine welcomes student birthdays in a special way. Enlarge, color, and cut out the gumball machine pattern on page 159; then post it on the board. Cut a small gumball from colorful construction paper for each child. Label the gumballs with student names and birthdays; then pin them inside the machine. Place a student's gumball in the slot on his birthday. Celebrate summer birthdays during the final days of the school year.

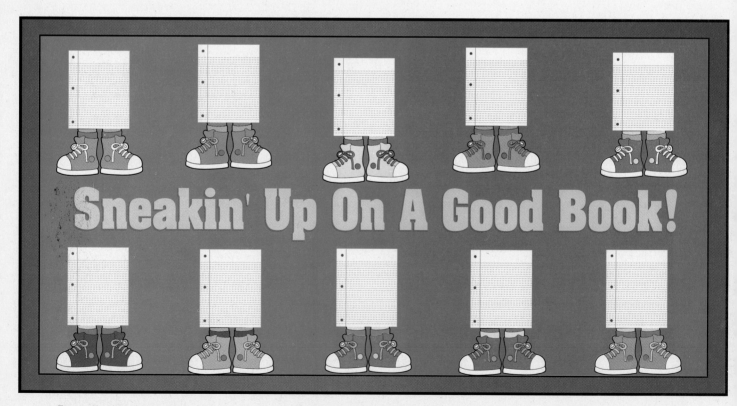

Sneakin' Up On A Good Book!

For a display that's got a lot of "sole," try this idea! Duplicate the sneaker patterns on page 161 on white paper for each child. A student colors and cuts out her sneakers; then she tapes them to the bottom of a brief book summary that she's written. Before you know it, students will be sneakin' a peek at this display and heading toward the library!

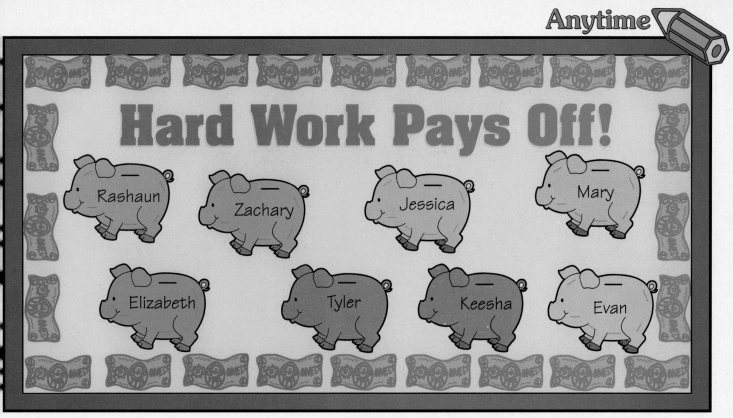

Hard Work Pays Off!

Rashaun

Zachary

Jessica

Mary

Elizabeth

Tyler

Keesha

Evan

Hard work pays off with this system of awards! Staple play money around the edges of the board for a fun border. Duplicate two copies of the piggy bank pattern on page 163 for each child. Each student cuts out his pair of piggies and staples them together to make a pocket. Pin the pockets on the board. Children earn play money to deposit in their banks for such accomplishments as attendance, good behavior, cooperation, and improved work. At the end of a week or month, have children count and trade their bucks for small rewards.

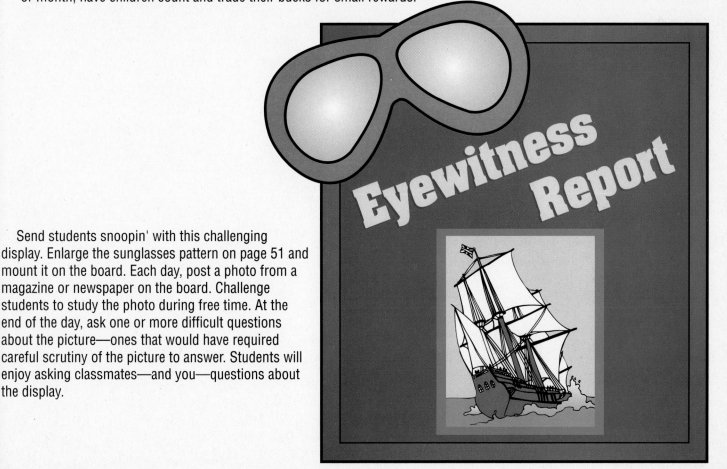

Eyewitness Report

Send students snoopin' with this challenging display. Enlarge the sunglasses pattern on page 51 and mount it on the board. Each day, post a photo from a magazine or newspaper on the board. Challenge students to study the photo during free time. At the end of the day, ask one or more difficult questions about the picture—ones that would have required careful scrutiny of the picture to answer. Students will enjoy asking classmates—and you—questions about the display.

 **Anytime**

Post this handy board to remind your class that classroom rules count! Enlarge the elephant pattern on page 61. After coloring and cutting out the elephant, curl its trunk around a pencil. Tie a bright ribbon around the trunk; then mount the elephant on the board. Cut cloud shapes from white paper and label them with classroom rules.

Don't Forget!

All work must be done in pencil and written in cursive.

Don't interrupt someone who is speaking.

Treat classmates as you would like to be treated.

All tests must be signed by a parent.

FICTION

NONFICTION

Good Books By The Bunch!

Encourage reading with this bulletin board challenge. Cut many small circles from purple and light green construction paper. Store the circles in envelopes stapled to the board. Attach two stems and two labels to the board as shown. When a student finishes a book, he writes its title and author on an appropriately colored circle and staples it to the board. Challenge students to keep reading until both bunches of grapes reach the bottom of the bulletin board.

Top Banana

Here's a fun twist to the student-of-the-week tradition. Enlarge the monkey on page 155. Color and cut out the pattern; then mount it on the board. Each Monday choose a student to be that week's "top banana." Have the child complete a copy of the form on page 165. Next have each child label a paper banana (pattern on page 167) with a positive comment about the "top banana." Add these to the display for a real self-esteem booster!

Get the scoop on school and classroom news all year long. Mount a large ice-cream cone and a scoop on a small bulletin board. Cut a slit in the scoop and insert a large paper clip. Write a special announcement or news item on a piece of construction paper; then clip it to the scoop. Change the news frequently, or assign the responsibility for collecting new "scoops" to student groups.

"Purr-fectly" Wonderful Cat Tales

This creative writing bulletin board is guaranteed to "cat-ch" your students' fancy! Have each student color and cut out a cat and cat tail (patterns on page 169) to attach to his completed "cat tale." Possible story starters include: "Turning into a cat seemed harmless until I...," "I nearly flipped when Catbo brought home a...," "My cat is so picky that...." Complete the display by adding a border of student-made paw prints.

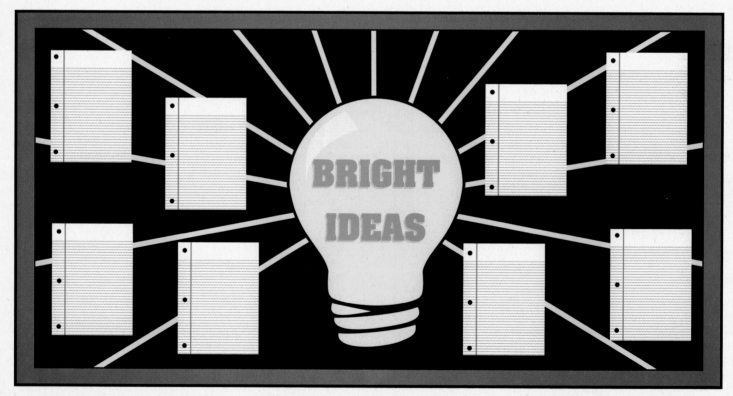

BRIGHT IDEAS

Shine a light on your students' bright ideas! Cover a bulletin board with black paper. Enlarge the light bulb pattern on page 139 on bright yellow paper; then cut it out, label it as shown, and mount it on the board. Add yellow yarn "rays." Have students brainstorm answers to questions such as "How can we improve our school?" and "Why do you think so many people don't vote in elections?"; then have them write their answers and add them to the display.

Put It Together With Books!

Puzzled about how to motivate children to read? Lay four large sheets of bulletin board paper (all different colors) on top of each other. Use paper clips to hold the sheets together. Draw four puzzle pieces on the top sheet; then cut all four sheets at once. Staple one puzzle piece of each color on the board as shown. (Save the remaining pieces for art projects.) Have each student draw a cover of a book he's read, glue the picture to a piece of tagboard, and cut it apart into puzzle pieces. Place each child's puzzle in a plastic bag and pin it to the board. Let students assemble each other's puzzles during free time.

Your students can "bone up" on science facts with this fun bulletin board. Enlarge the dog pattern on page 171. Duplicate the bone pattern on white paper. Write science facts, review questions, or vocabulary words on the bones; then cut them out. Use this bulletin board to introduce a unit or as a review. Change the title and make more bones to adapt the display to other subject areas or skills.

Boning Up On Science

seed

stem

pistil

stamen

roots

flowers

pollen

Help your students pat themselves on the backs for a job well done! Have each child trace his hand on a piece of construction paper and cut out the tracing. On the cutout, have the student write something that he has recently learned or a skill on which he has improved. Encourage social, athletic, and artistic accomplishments as well as academic achievements. Staple the "applauding" hands around the board's title.

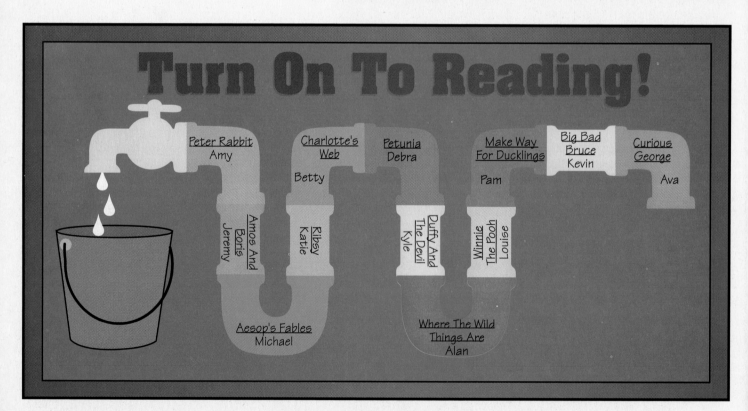

Keep a record of the books that your students read with this colorful pipeline. Staple a large bucket cutout to the board. Duplicate the faucet and pipe pieces on pages 173 and 175 on colorful pieces of construction paper. After reading a book, a student selects a pattern, cuts it out, labels it with the title of the book and his name, and adds it to the pipeline. Students will love the chance to choose the direction the pipeline will take!

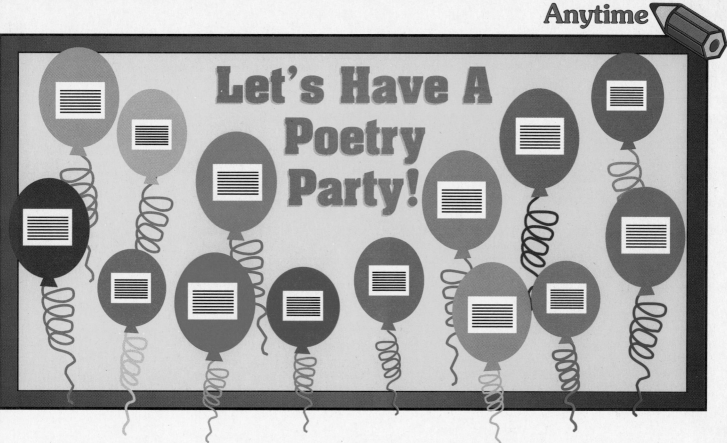

Let's Have A Poetry Party!

Celebrate your students' poetry with a colorful party display! Cut several balloons in assorted sizes and colors from construction paper. Mount the balloons and your students' poetry on the bulletin board. Cut balloon strings from colorful curling ribbon and attach them to the balloons.

Follow Your Guide

fan
grow
green

lucky
now

ask
blue

red
snow
robin

tell
will

Turn a bulletin board into a learning center on dictionary usage. Mount a large mountain cutout on a bulletin board. Duplicate five copies of the guide pattern on page 177 on white paper. Have student volunteers color the guides, cut them out, and staple them to the mountain. Write a guide word pair on each guide's pack; then insert a pushpin below the pack. Label small cards with entry words. Punch a hole in the top of each card. Store the cards in a pocket attached to the board. Have students remove the cards and hang each one on the correct guide.

We Think You're Just Ducky!

Matthew

Let this flock of feathered friends boost self-esteem! Enlarge the pattern on page 179; color, laminate, and cut it out before posting it on the board. Add a few cut-out raindrops to the display. Duplicate a duck pattern (also on page 179) on yellow paper for each child. Each Monday use a wipe-off marker to write a child's name on the umbrella. Have students label their duck cutouts with positive comments about the honored child. Wipe the umbrella clean at the end of the week, duplicate more ducks, and you'll be ready for Monday!

Looking for a simple way to celebrate National Book Week or motivate reading all year long? Try a book quilt! Give each child a square of white paper. On the paper the student illustrates his favorite book, writing the book's title and author somewhere on his drawing. Mount the drawings on a large, colorful piece of bulletin board paper. Use a black marker to add "stitches" around each square to create a quilted effect.

Our Book Quilt

Help your students enjoy the sweet taste of success with this incentive display. Enlarge the gumball machine pattern on page 159. After coloring and cutting it out, mount the machine on a small bulletin board. Cut out a large circle from construction paper for each child. Label the gumballs with students' names and staple them on the board as shown. Each time a student improves in a skill, scores well on a test, or reaches a goal, he gets a sticker to place on his gumball. When five stickers have been earned, the student receives a special prize.

The "faces in a crowd" that adorn this board make it an outrageously appealing display! Have each child draw and cut out an illustration of his face and a speech bubble labeled with a positive phrase. Mount these cutouts around the edges of a bulletin board. Duplicate the star pattern on page 101 on yellow paper for each child. Label the stars with students' names; then display them with papers selected by your students.

45

We've Done Some Rootin'-Tootin' Terrific Things!

Recognize the hard work of your young buckaroos with this rootin'-tootin' display! Enlarge and color the cowboy pattern on page 181; then cut it out and mount it on the board. For fun, pin a real bandana kerchief on the cowboy. Duplicate the hat pattern on page 183 on construction paper for each child. A student cuts out her hat; then she labels it with her name and one or two sentences about a rootin'-tootin' terrific thing she's done.

Investigate A New Book

Send students on the trail of a good book! Enlarge and color the detective pattern on page 185; then cut it out and mount it on the board. Duplicate the magnifying glass on page 187 on construction paper for each child. From notebook paper, have the student cut out a circle that is slightly smaller than the magnifying glass. The child glues the notebook paper circle on his magnifying glass; then he labels it with a brief summary of a book he has just read. Place a basket of mystery books near the display to whet your detectives' reading appetites!

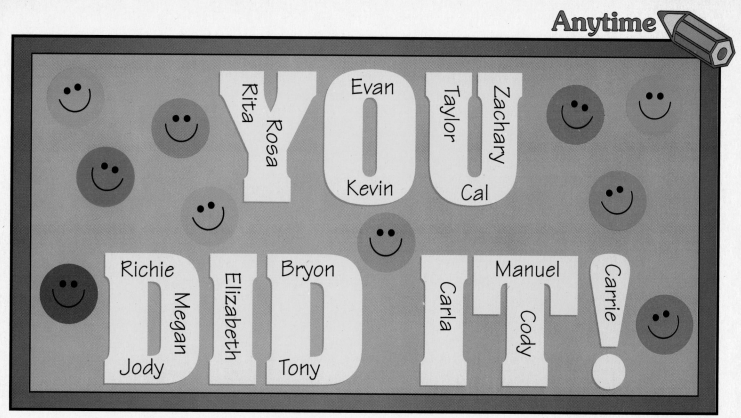

Not every child is capable of being an A student—for some, getting a C is a great accomplishment! Cut the letters "YOU DID IT!" from large sheets of construction paper. Mount the letters on a bulletin board along with some colorful happy faces. Assign a letter to each child. Explain that you will write "YOU DID IT!" on the paper of any student who you think did his or her best. When a child receives a "YOU DID IT!" paper back, he gets to sign his name on his letter. With this giant display as a reminder, students will soon learn that anything is possible if they try!

Reeling in good work is a snap with this clever display! Purchase an inexpensive fishnet (available at party supply stores) and attach it to the board as shown. Fill the net with samples of student work. Have each child place one hand, palm down, on a sheet of construction paper; then have him trace, cut out, and decorate the shape to resemble a fish. Mount the fish with a few water plant cutouts for a "fin-tastic" display!

Reading Makes Good "Cents"!

Fiction = 25¢
Nonfiction = 30¢
Poetry = 40¢
Biography = 50¢

You can bank on the reading motivation provided by this fun display! Staple a border of play money around a bulletin board's edges. Enlarge the pattern on page 163. Color it and add a slot at the top before cutting out the pig; then label the pig as shown and mount it on the board. Duplicate the pig pattern on colorful paper for each child. Have students cut out their pigs, sign them, and add them to the board. When a student reads a book, use a coin stamp to stamp the appropriate amount on his bank. Award prizes to students when their stamps total $1.00.

Here's another piggy board that's packed with learning! Make a large pig as described in the preceding idea. (Leave off the slot at the top.) Laminate the pig. Each week use a wipe-off marker to program the cutout with bonus spelling words. Have student groups use dictionaries to find the meanings of the words and write sentences using them. At the end of the week, review the words; then wipe the piggy clean so it's ready for next week's words! For fun, let your students suggest words to write on the piggy.

To encourage reading, decorate the background of a bulletin board to resemble a door. Have students trace their hands on yellow paper, cut out the tracings, and label the cutouts with their names. Duplicate the key pattern on page 189 on pastel construction paper for each child. Have students write brief book summaries on their keys before mounting them on the board with the hand cutouts as shown.

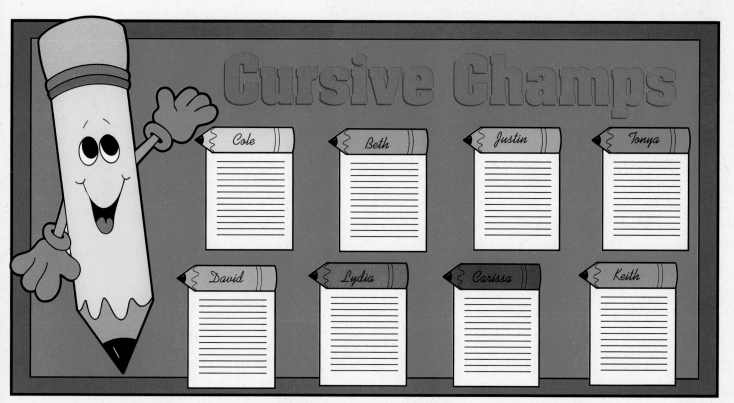

Motivate students to improve their cursive writing with an appealing display. Enlarge the animated pencil pattern on page 191. After coloring and cutting it out, mount the pencil on the board. Duplicate the student pencil pattern on page 191 on construction paper for each child. Have students cut out their pencils and mount them on the board with samples of their best cursive writing. Encourage students to continue posting improved writing samples on the board.

Use with "I've Got A Hunch This Is A Bright Bunch!" on page 3 and "Eyewitness Report" on page 37.

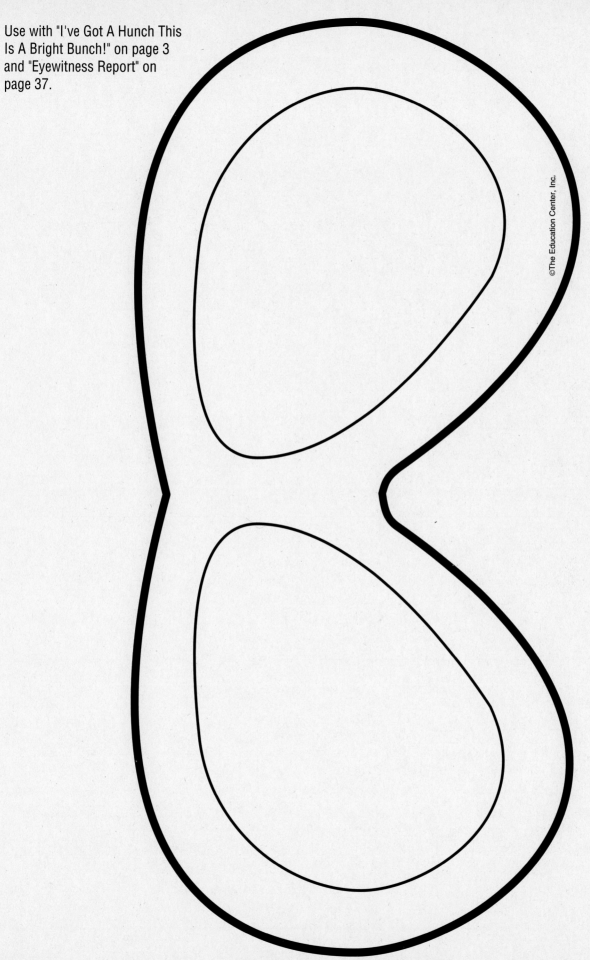

©The Education Center, Inc.

©1992 The Education Center, Inc., Greensboro, NC

Use with "My New Class Suits Me To A 'T'!" on page 3 and "It Was A 'Tee-rific' Summer" on page 6.

©1992 The Education Center, Inc.

Use with "My 'Beary' Special Students" on page 4.

©1992 The Education Center, Inc., Greensboro, NC

Use with "I'm So 'Hoppy' You Are Here!" on page 4.

Enlarge.

©1992 The Education Center, Inc., Greensboro, NC

Use the flower pattern with "Plant Yourself Here!" on page 5 and "Flowers And Showers" on page 28.

Use the flowerpot pattern with "Plant Yourself Here!" on page 5.

Enlarge it to use with "My Class Has A Lot Of Heart!" on page 23.

©1992 The Education Center, Inc., Greensboro, NC

Enlarge and use with "I Can't Forget Summer! Can You?" on page 6 and "Don't Forget!" on page 38.

©1992 The Education Center, Inc., Greensboro, NC

Use with "Doing A Whale Of A Job!" on page 7.

©1992 The Education Center, Inc., Greensboro, NC

Use with "Pitch In!" on page 7.

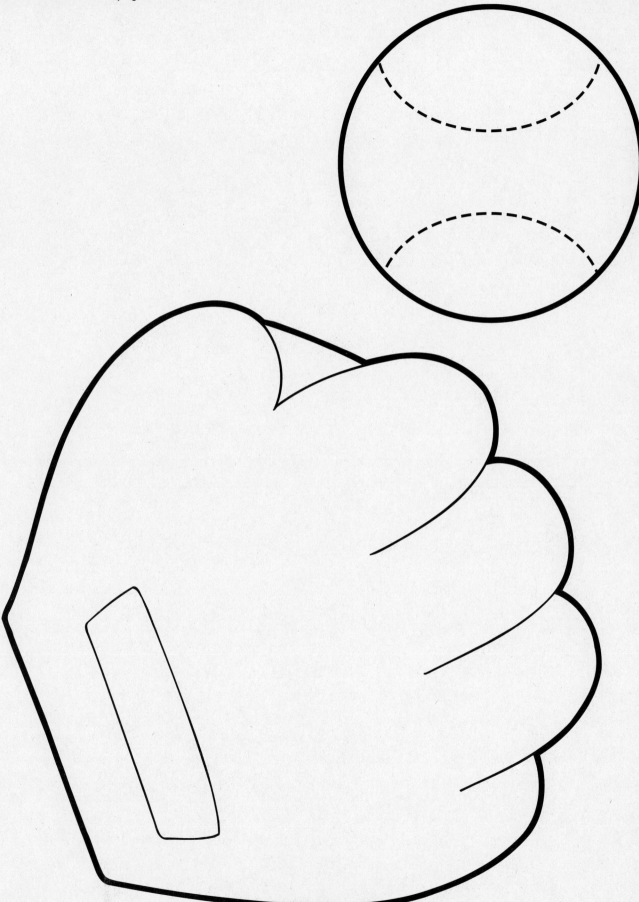

©1992 The Education Center, Inc., Greensboro, NC

Use with "An Autumn Rainbow Of Great Work" on page 8 and "Check These Out!" on page 9.

©1992 The Education Center, Inc., Greensboro, NC

Use with "Poppin' Good Papers!" on page 8.

Paper Topper

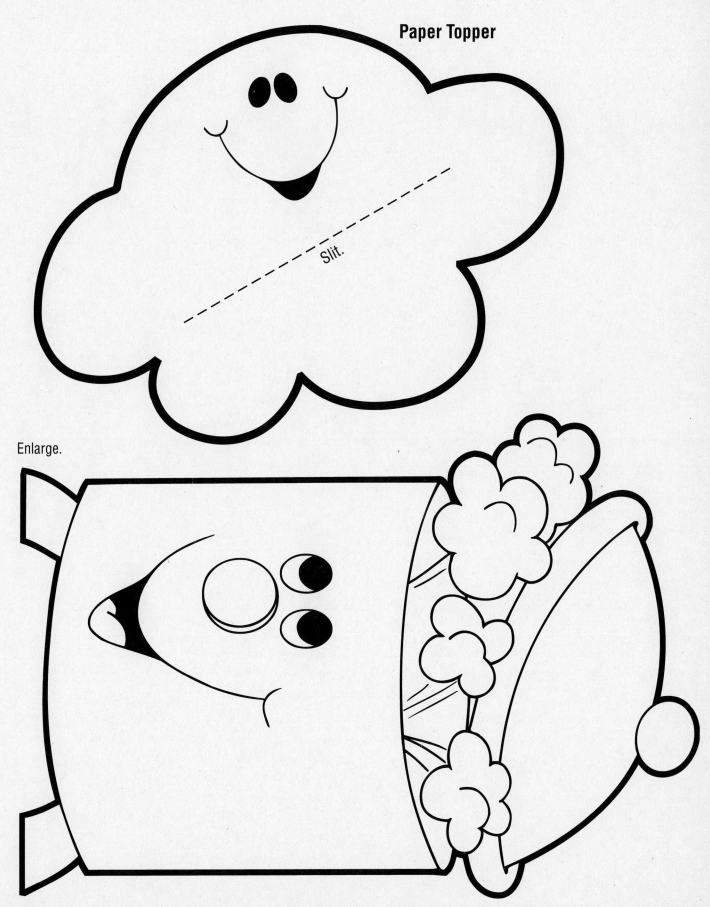

Slit.

Enlarge.

©1992 The Education Center, Inc., Greensboro, NC

Enlarge and use with "We're Just Nuts About You!" on page 9.

©1992 The Education Center, Inc., Greensboro, NC

Use with "We're Just Nuts About You!" on page 9.

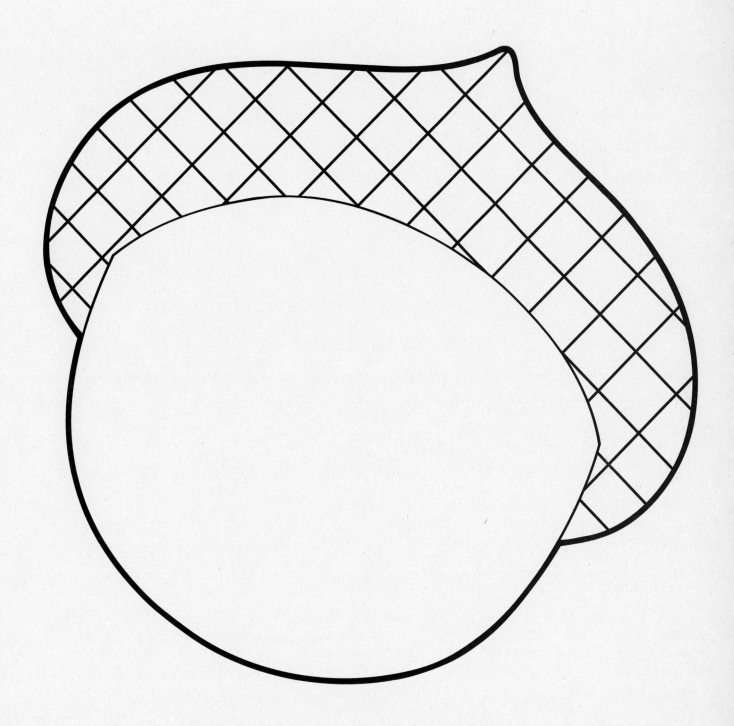

©1992 The Education Center, Inc., Greensboro, NC

Enlarge and use with "Haunted Helpers" on page 10.

R.I.P.

©1992 The Education Center, Inc., Greensboro, NC

Use with "Pumpkin Personalities" on page 11.

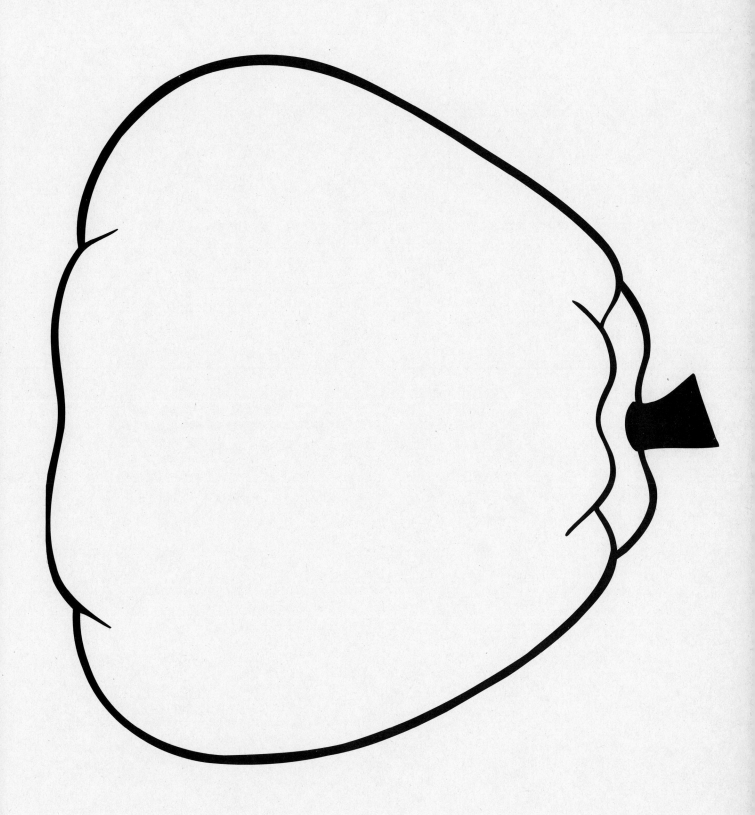

©1992 The Education Center, Inc., Greensboro, NC

Enlarge and use with "I'm Thankful For You!" on page 12.

©1992 The Education Center, Inc., Greensboro, NC

Enlarge and use with "Gobblin' Good Behavior" on page 13.

©1992 The Education Center, Inc., Greensboro, NC

Use with "We're Counting Our Blessings!" on page 13.

©1992 The Education Center, Inc.

Use with "Gifts From The Heart" on page 14, "Love Bug To The Rescue!" on page 22, and "How About A Sweetheart Shake?" on page 23.

Use with "...And A Partridge In A Pear Tree" on page 15. (Enlarge if desired.)

©1992 The Education Center, Inc., Greensboro, NC

Use with "...And A Partridge In A Pear Tree" on page 15. (Enlarge if desired.)

©1992 The Education Center, Inc., Greensboro, NC

Use with "…And A Partridge In A Pear Tree" on page 15. (Enlarge if desired.)

©1992 The Education Center, Inc., Greensboro, NC

Use with "...And A Partridge In A Pear Tree" on page 15. (Enlarge if desired.)

©1992 The Education Center, Inc., Greensboro, NC

Enlarge and use with "Santa's Workshop" on page 17.

©1992 The Education Center, Inc., Greensboro, NC

Use with "Star of David..." on page 17.

Enlarge.

©1992 The Education Center, Inc., Greensboro, NC

Enlarge and use with "When You Wish Upon A Star..." on page 18.

©1992 The Education Center, Inc., Greensboro, NC

Use with "When You Wish Upon A Star..." on page 18 and "Outrageously Outstanding!" on page 45.

©1992 The Education Center, Inc., Greensboro, NC

Enlarge and use with "Light A Candle For Peace" on page 19.

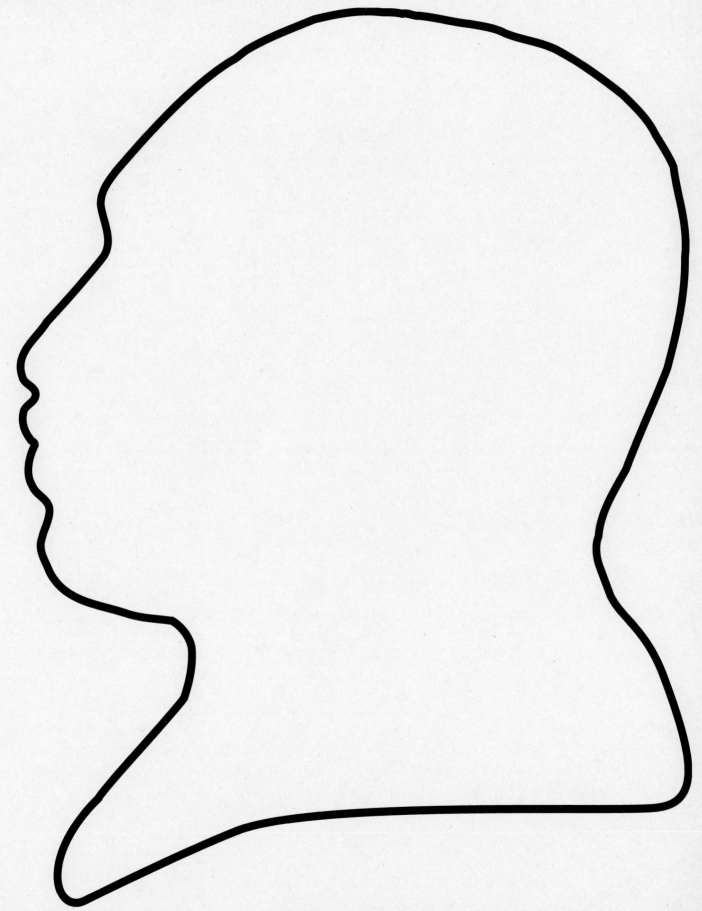

©1992 The Education Center, Inc., Greensboro, NC

Use with "They Made Their Mark!" on page 19.

©1992 The Education Center, Inc., Greensboro, NC

Enlarge and use with "Winter Writing Wonderland" on page 20.

©1992 The Education Center, Inc., Greensboro, NC

Use with "Winter Writing Wonderland" on page 20.

©1992 The Education Center, Inc.

Patterns

Use with "Love One Another" on page 22, "My Class Has A Lot Of Heart!" on page 23, and "Books Take You Over The Rainbow" on page 26.

©1992 The Education Center, Inc., Greensboro, NC

Enlarge and use with "How About A Sweetheart Shake?" on page 23.

©1992 The Education Center, Inc., Greensboro, NC

Enlarge and use with "Good For 'Ewe'!" on page 24.

©1992 The Education Center, Inc., Greensboro, NC

Enlarge and use with "Grade A Readers" on page 24.

Grade A Readers

©1992 The Education Center, Inc., Greensboro, NC

Use with "Reading Is 'Toad-ally' Awesome!" on page 25.

©1992 The Education Center, Inc., Greensboro, NC

Use with "Spring Is In The Air!" on page 25.

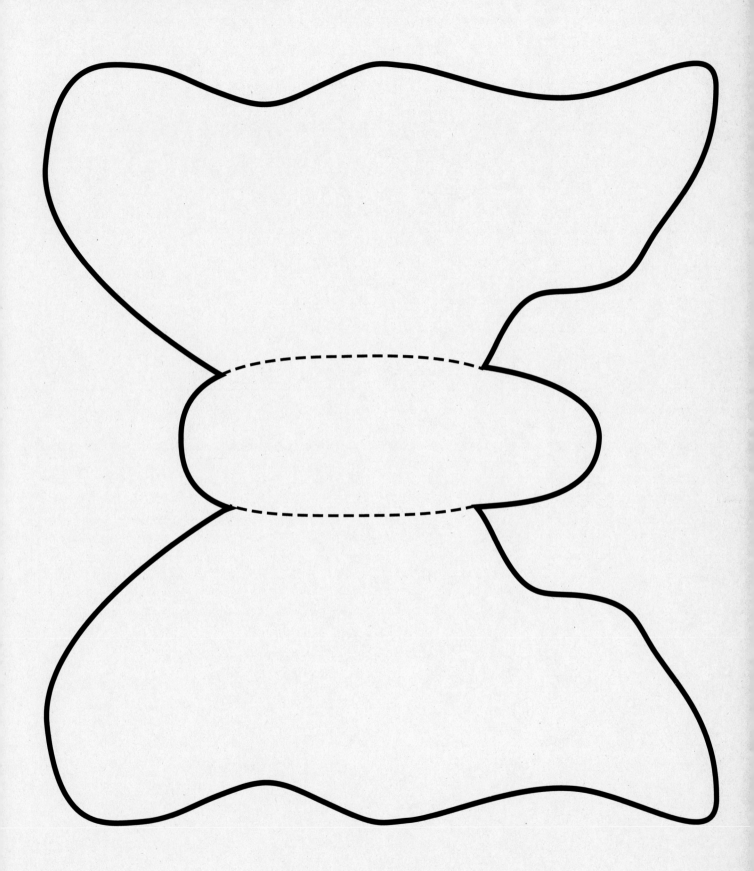

©1992 The Education Center, Inc., Greensboro, NC

Enlarge and use with "Books Take You Over The Rainbow" on page 26.

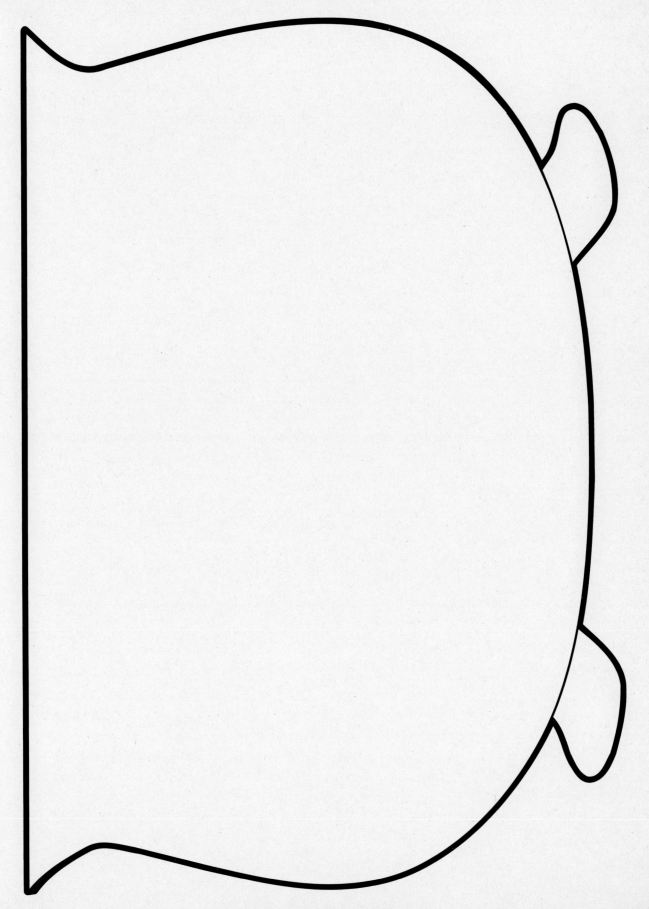

©1992 The Education Center, Inc., Greensboro, NC

Enlarge and use with "Irish Potato Plots" on page 26.

©1992 The Education Center, Inc., Greensboro, NC

Use with "Irish Potato Plots" on page 26.

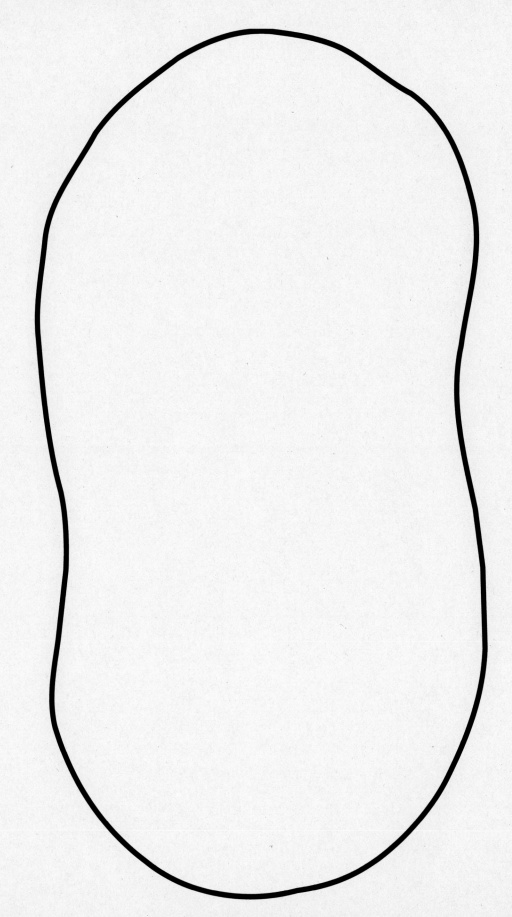

©1992 The Education Center, Inc., Greensboro, NC

Enlarge and use with " 'Egg-stra' Special" on page 27.

©1992 The Education Center, Inc., Greensboro, NC

Use with "Bunny Tales" on page 27. Duplicate the large pattern on pink paper. Duplicate the small pattern on white paper.

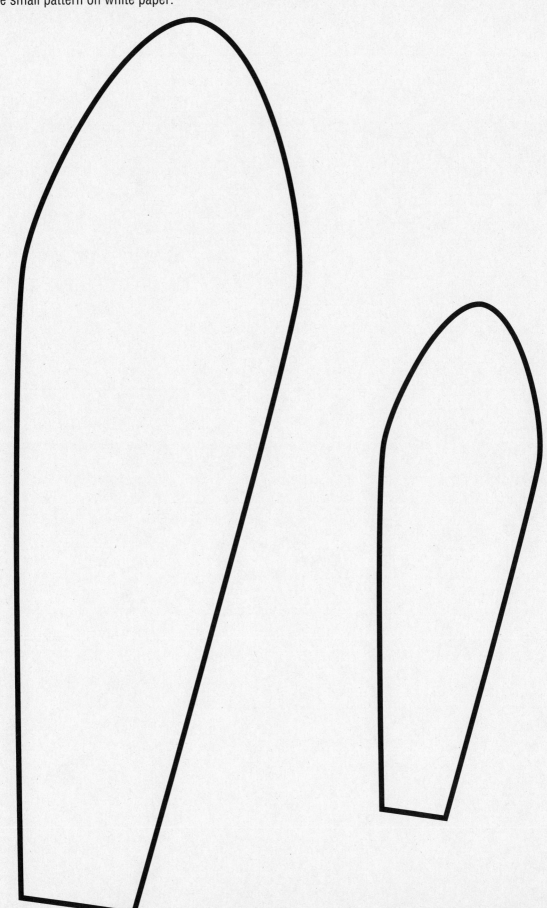

©1992 The Education Center, Inc., Greensboro, NC

Patterns

Enlarge the umbrella pattern to use with "Flowers And Showers" on page 28.

Use the bee pattern with "It's Been A 'Bee-utiful' Year!" on page 29.

©1992 The Education Center, Inc., Greensboro, NC

133

Enlarge and use with "Let's End The Year With A Bang!" on page 29.

©1992 The Education Center, Inc., Greensboro, NC

Use with "We Had A Bushel Of Fun This Year!" on page 30.

©1992 The Education Center, Inc., Greensboro, NC

Use with "Highlights Of The Year" on page 30. Enlarge to use with "Bright Ideas" on page 40.

©1992 The Education Center, Inc., Greensboro, NC

Use with "Color Your World With Books!" on page 31.

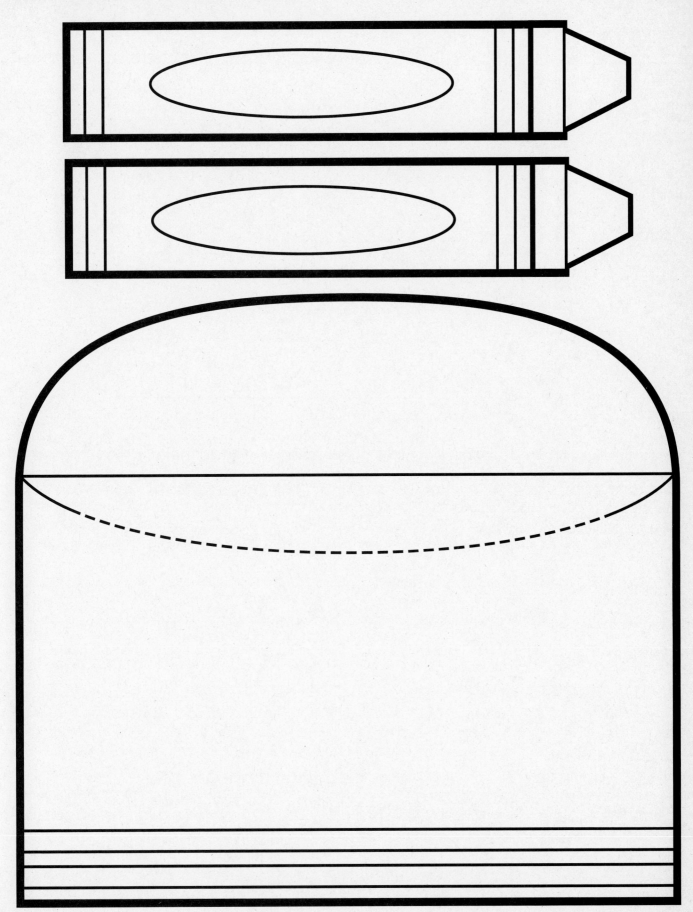

©1992 The Education Center, Inc., Greensboro, NC

Enlarge and use with "The Cat's Out Of The Bag!" on page 31.

©1992 The Education Center, Inc., Greensboro, NC

Use with "Home Sweet Home" on page 32.

©1992 The Education Center, Inc., Greensboro, NC

Enlarge and use with " 'Fan-tastic' Work!" on page 33.

©1992 The Education Center, Inc., Greensboro, NC

Enlarge and use with "Some Extra Time?" on page 33.

©1992 The Education Center, Inc., Greensboro, NC

Use with "Right On Target!" on page 34.

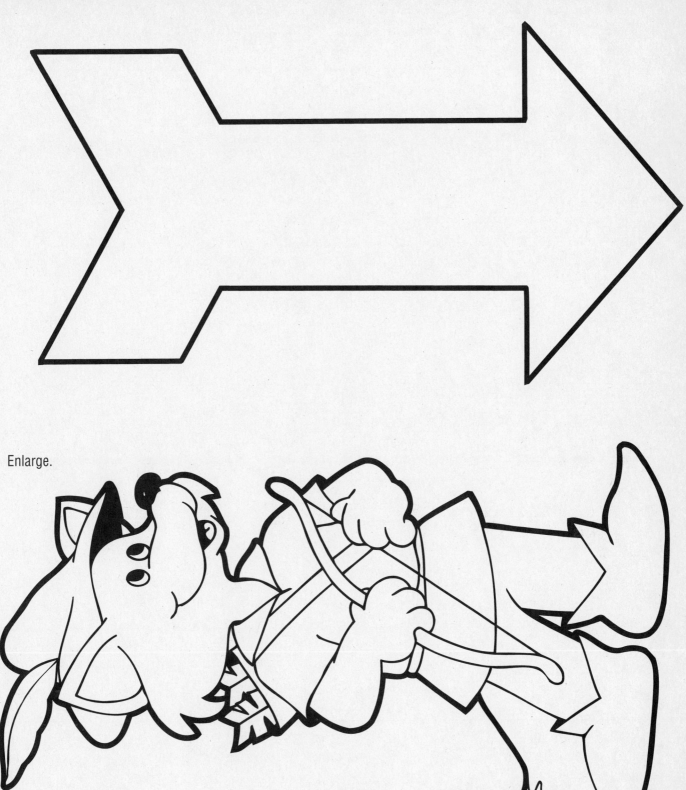

Enlarge.

©1992 The Education Center, Inc., Greensboro, NC

Use with "Who Are You Going To Call?" on page 34.

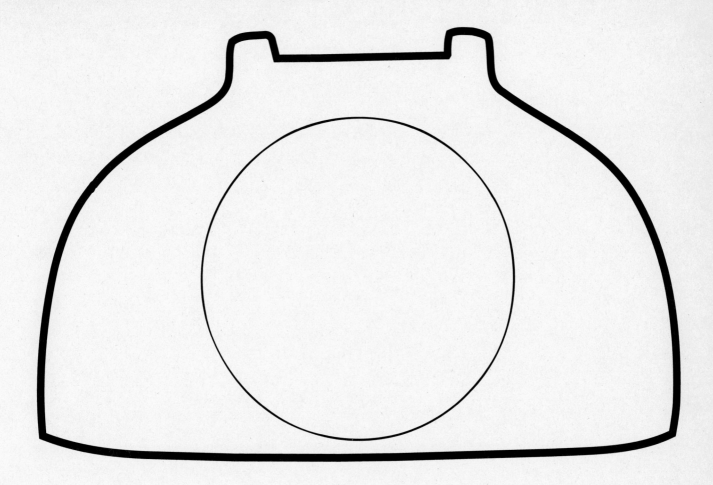

©1992 The Education Center, Inc., Greensboro, NC

Use with "Don't Monkey Around!" on page 35 and "Top Banana" on page 39.

Enlarge.

Paper Topper

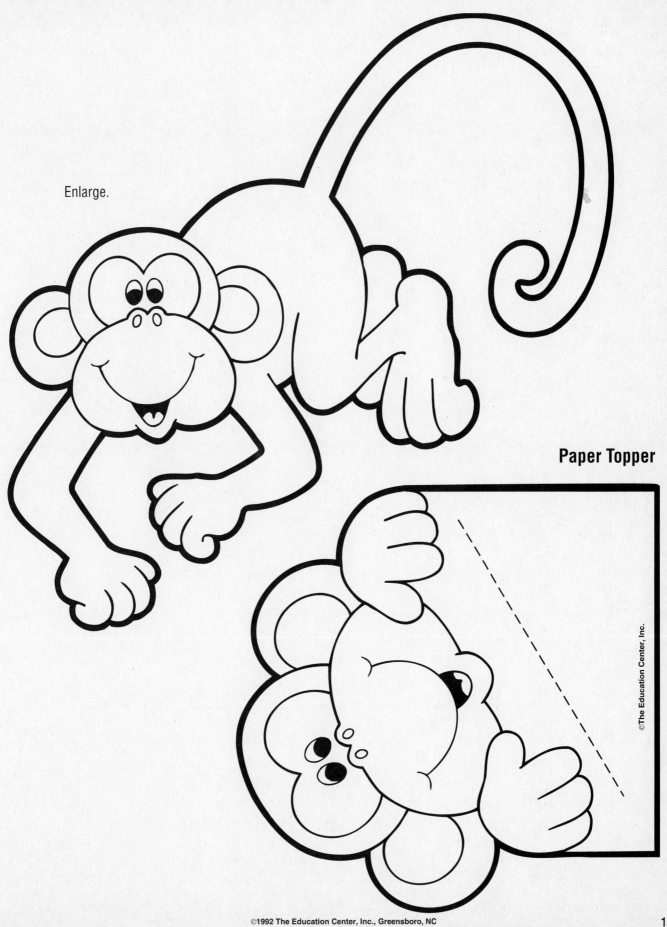

© The Education Center, Inc.

Use with "Flying High With Spelling" on page 35.

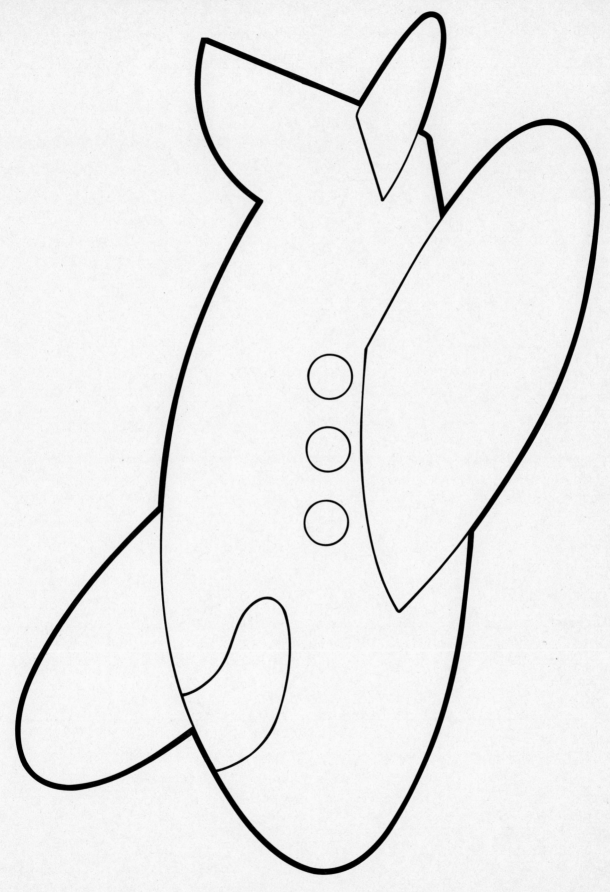

©1992 The Education Center, Inc., Greensboro, NC

Enlarge and use with "Goody, Goody Gumball! It's Your Birthday!" on page 36 and "We're On The Ball!" on page 45.

©1992 The Education Center, Inc., Greensboro, NC

Use with "Sneakin' Up On A Good Book!" on page 36.

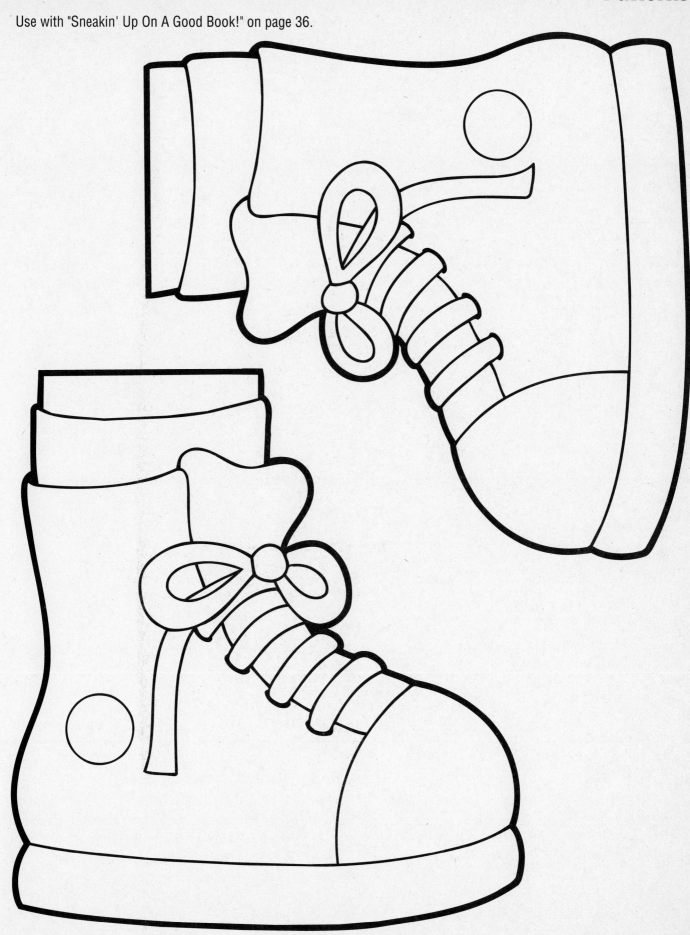

©1992 The Education Center, Inc., Greensboro, NC

Use with "Hard Work Pays Off!" on page 37 and "Reading Makes Good 'Cents'!" and "This Little Piggy Went To The Dictionary!" on page 48.

©1992 The Education Center, Inc., Greensboro, NC

This week's Top Banana is

_____.

Here's some "ap-peel-ing" information about the Top Banana:

1. My favorite food is _____.

2. My favorite school subject is _____.

3. My least favorite school subject is _____.

4. A career I'd like in the future is _____ because

   _____.

5. When I'm with my friends, I really like to _____

   _____.

6. When I'm alone, my favorite thing to do is _____

   _____.

7. My favorite TV show is _____.

8. I think that the best color in the world is _____.

9. One thing I do really well is _____.

10. The best thing about me is _____

   _____.

©1992 The Education Center, Inc., Greensboro, NC

Use with "Top Banana" on page 39.

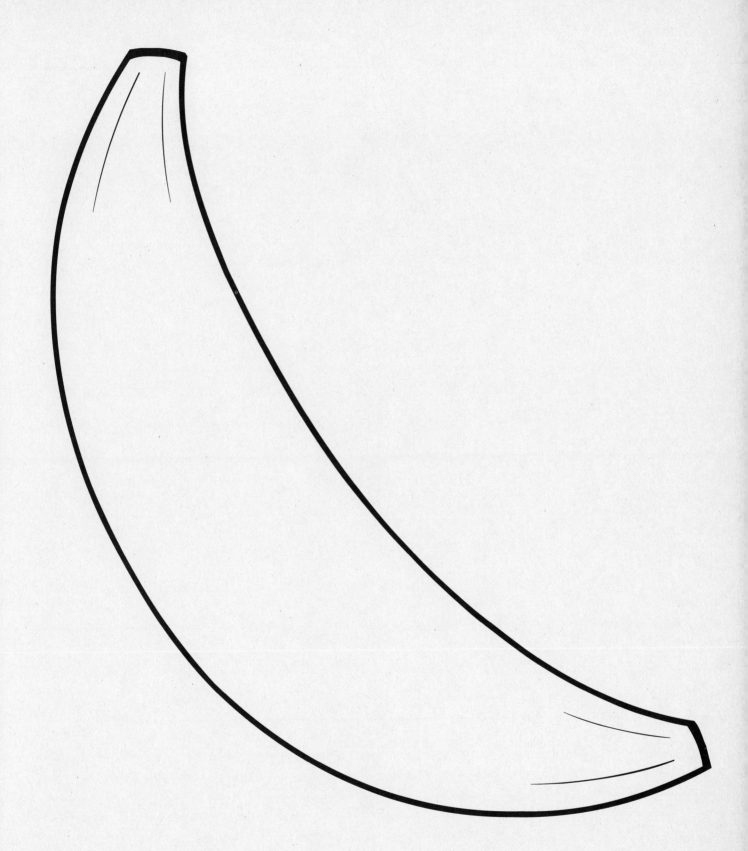

©1992 The Education Center, Inc., Greensboro, NC

Use with " 'Purr-fectly' Wonderful Cat Tales" on page 40. Cut on the dotted lines.

©1992 The Education Center, Inc., Greensboro, NC

Use with "Boning Up On Science" on page 41.

Enlarge.

©1992 The Education Center, Inc., Greensboro, NC

Use with "Turn On To Reading!" on page 42.

©1992 The Education Center, Inc., Greensboro, NC

Use with "Turn On To Reading!" on page 42.

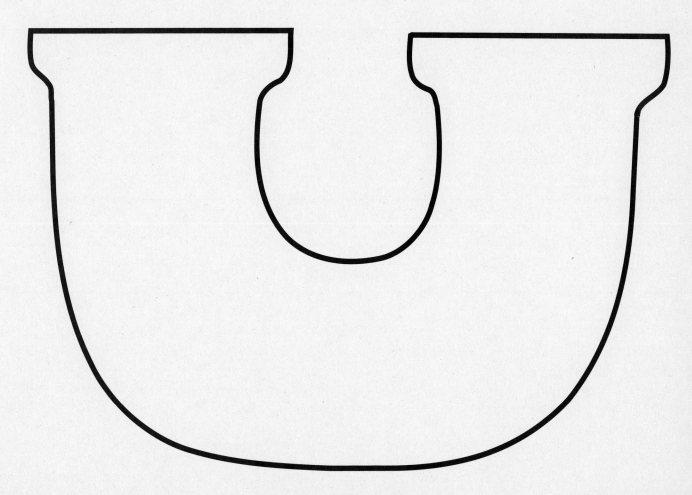

©1992 The Education Center, Inc., Greensboro, NC

Use with "Follow Your Guide" on page 43.

Pattern

©1992 The Education Center, Inc., Greensboro, NC

Use with "We Think You're Just Ducky!" on page 44.

Enlarge.

©1992 The Education Center, Inc., Greensboro, NC

Enlarge and use with "We've Done Some Rootin'-Tootin' Terrific Things!" on page 46.

©1992 The Education Center, Inc., Greensboro, NC

Use with "We've Done Some Rootin'-Tootin' Terrific Things!" on page 46.

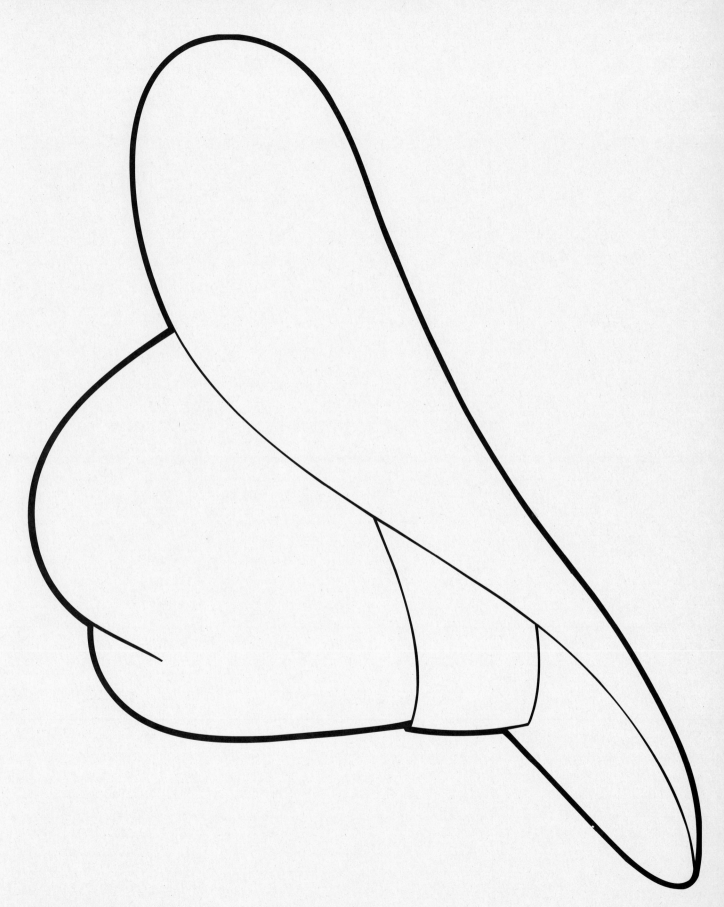

©1992 The Education Center, Inc., Greensboro, NC

Enlarge and use with "Investigate A New Book" on page 46.

©1992 The Education Center, Inc., Greensboro, NC

Use with "Investigate A New Book" on page 46.

©1992 The Education Center, Inc., Greensboro, NC

Use with "Reading Unlocks The World's Doors" on page 49.

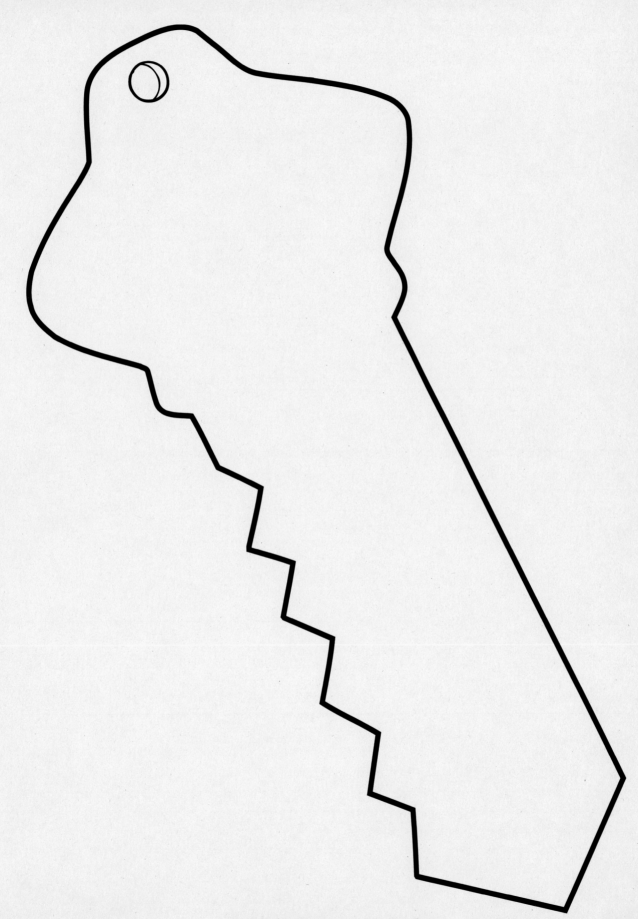

©1992 The Education Center, Inc., Greensboro, NC